Indigenous Peoples

Written by Robin Koontz

rourkeeducationalmedia.com

*Scan for Related Titles
and Teacher Resources*

www.rourkeeducationalmedia.com

PHOTO CREDITS: Cover: © Mlenny Photography; title page: © Bartosz Hadyniak; page 5: © The Power of Forever Photography; page 7: © Pecold; page 9: © Britta Kasholm-Tengve; page 12: © Americanspirit; page 13: © Tony Laidig; page 15: © Coral Coolahan; page 17: © Antonella865; page 19: © Wdeon; page 20: © MShep2, © Bartosz Hadyniak; page 21: © Bartosz Hadyniak

Edited by: Precious McKenzie

Cover and Interior design by: Tara Raymo

Library of Congress PCN Data

Indigenous Peoples / Robin Koontz
(Little World Social Studies)
ISBN 978-1-62169-915-6 (hard cover)(alk. paper)
ISBN 978-1-62169-810-4 (soft cover)
ISBN 978-1-62717-020-8 (e-Book)
Library of Congress Control Number: 2013937309

Also Available as:
ROURKE'S
e-Books

Rourke Educational Media
Printed in the United States of America,
North Mankato, Minnesota

Rourke
Educational Media
rourkeeducationalmedia.com
customerservice@rourkeeducationalmedia.com • PO Box 643328 Vero Beach, Florida 32964

Table of Contents

The First People

It happened thousands of years ago. A group of people settled in a place where no one had ever lived. These first people are called **indigenous** peoples.

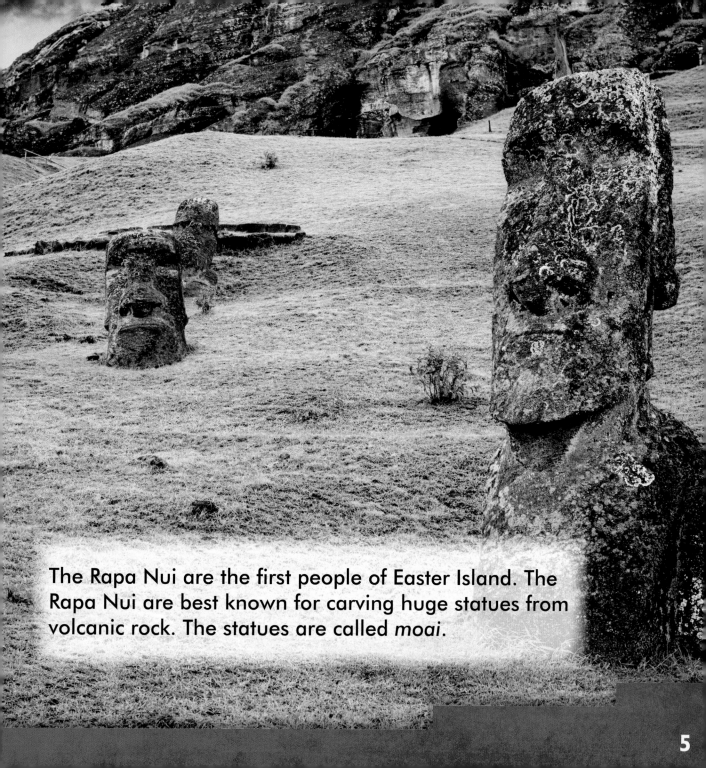

The Rapa Nui are the first people of Easter Island. The Rapa Nui are best known for carving huge statues from volcanic rock. The statues are called *moai*.

Indigenous peoples are also called first peoples, tribal peoples, or First Nations. They live all over the world.

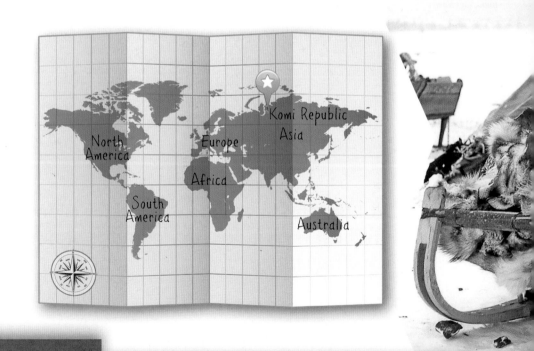

Komi reindeer herders are indigenous peoples who still live by the old ways on the cold northern coast of Russia.

Native people live in harmony with the Earth. They might have a **traditional** language and style of dress. They have special ways to survive.

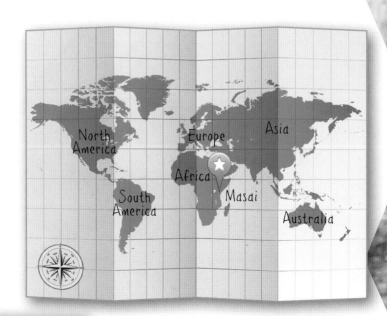

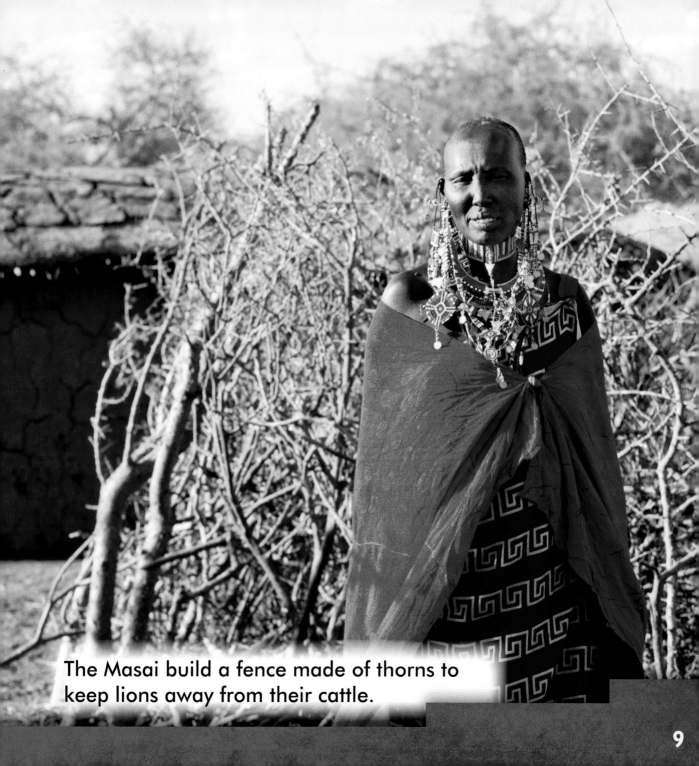

The Masai build a fence made of thorns to keep lions away from their cattle.

A Time of Change

Long ago, new people arrived in places where indigenous peoples lived. The new people **colonized** the native land.

North America

Europe

Asia

Africa

South America

Australia

Indigenous Peoples

The red on this map shows where indigenous peoples are living today.

In North America, the arrival of Europeans changed the lives of Native Americans.

Members of the Cherokee Nation, in the United States, have been weaving baskets the same way for thousands of years.

Preserving Heritage

Indigenous peoples **preserve** their cultural **heritage** and their language by teaching the younger generations about them.

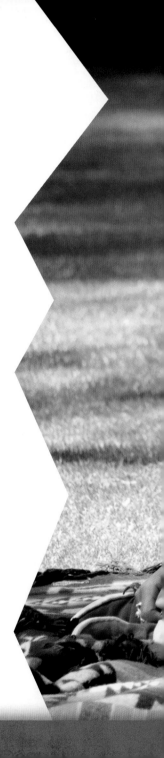

Many indigenous peoples continue to use wild foods and medicines that their families used before them. It's one way they can preserve their **culture**.

In North America, pow wows are a celebration of Native American traditions. Some tribes open their pow wows to the public to teach others about their culture.

Indigenous peoples protected the Earth for all of us for thousands of years. Now it's our turn to help preserve the first people's identity and their land.

Many groups are helping indigenous peoples preserve their culture and traditions so their history is not forgotten.

Picture Glossary

 **colonized** (KOL-ih-nized): People colonize when they start or form a colony somewhere. Then that place has been colonized.

 **culture** (KUHL-chur): The beliefs, customs, traditions, and way of life for a group of people.

 **heritage** (HARE-ih-tij): Heritage is what comes from someone's background.

indigenous (in-DIJ-uh-nuhss): Someone is indigenous when they are native to the place where they live. Plants and animals can also be indigenous.

preserve (pri-ZURV): To preserve means to keep something safe.

traditional (truh-DISH-uh-nuhl): Traditional relates to the customs and ways of doing things. Traditions become part of a culture and are passed to the children.

Index

Websites

www.nativeplanet.org/index.shtml

www.un.org/Pubs/CyberSchoolBus/indigenous/index.asp

www.culturalsurvival.org

About the Author

Robin Koontz is an author/illustrator of a wide variety of books and articles for children and young adults. She lives with her husband in the Coast Range of western Oregon.

Meet The Author!
www.meetREMauthors.com